Engineering Our World

How a
Computer
Is Made

By Sam Aloian

Gareth Stevens
PUBLISHING

Please visit our website, www.garethstevens.com. For a free color catalog of all our high-quality books, call toll free 1-800-542-2595 or fax 1-877-542-2596.

Library of Congress Cataloging-in-Publication Data

Aloian, Sam, author.
 How a computer is made / Sam Aloian.
    pages cm. — (Engineering our world)
 Includes bibliographical references and index.
ISBN 978-1-4824-3927-4 (pbk.)
ISBN 978-1-4824-3928-1 (6 pack)
ISBN 978-1-4824-3929-8 (library binding)
1. Electronic digital computers—Design and construction—Juvenile literature. 2. Computers—Juvenile literature. I. Title.
 QA76.52.A46 2016
 004—dc23

2015032502

First Edition

Published in 2016 by
Gareth Stevens Publishing
111 East 14th Street, Suite 349
New York, NY 10003

Copyright © 2016 Gareth Stevens Publishing

Designer: Samantha DeMartin
Editor: Ryan Nagelhout

Photo credits: Cover, p. 1 jannoon028/Shutterstock.com; caption box stoonn/Shutterstock.com; background Jason Winter/Shutterstock.com; p. 5 US Army/Science Source/Getty Images; p. 7 (keyboard) rangizzz/Shutterstock.com; p. 7 (apps) Oleksiy Mark/Shutterstock.com; p. 7 (monitor) robert_s/Shutterstock.com; p. 7 (OS) Dukes/Shutterstock.com; p. 7 (coding) Semisatch/Shutterstock.com; p. 9 Ana Vasileva/Shutterstock.com; p. 11 Bacho/Shutterstock.com; p. 12 ChicagoStockPhotography/Shutterstock.com; p. 13 Piotr Tomicki/Shutterstock.com; p. 15 Denis Dryashkin/Shutterstock.com; p. 17 vtwinpixel/Shutterstock.com; p. 19 bibiphoto/Shutterstock.com; p. 20 (hand) Everything/Shutterstock.com; p. 20 (keys) DVARG/Shutterstock.com; p. 21 (boy) Greg da Silva/Shutterstock.com; p. 21 (wire) cherezoff/Shutterstock.com.

Printed in the United States of America

CPSIA compliance information: Batch #CW16GS: For further information contact Gareth Stevens, New York, New York at 1-800-542-2595.

Contents

Words in the glossary appear in **bold** type the first time they are used in the text.

Wires and Wonders

The first computers were as big as entire rooms, but today the parts we need to build a computer can fit in your hand. Phones, tablets, and other **electronics** are all tiny computers **designed** to do many different jobs.

But making these superfast machines work isn't easy. All computers are made of similar parts and follow a similar process to go from wires and chips to wonderful **devices** we use every day. Let's find out how to build a computer!

Building Blocks

The first general purpose computer was called ENIAC. Built between 1943 and 1945, it took up 1,500 square feet (139 sq m)! Today's computers are much smaller and much more powerful!

The ENIAC—**E**lectronic **N**umerical **I**ntegrator **A**nd **C**omputer—worked much differently than today's computers. Can you imagine needing a computer the size of a room?

5

Hard and Soft

Computer **engineers** use their training in both engineering and computer science to build computers. Computers work thanks to two different kinds of inventions. Hardware is the name for the pieces of the computer itself. Software, meanwhile, is the **programming** needed to do tasks on the computer. Software is made of lines of **code** stored on the computer's memory.

Hardware and software engineers work together to make sure the computer works properly.

Building Blocks

The program that runs the entire computer, called the operating system (OS), is the most important piece of coding on a computer. Without it, you can't use the computer at all.

Some software needs certain kinds of hardware to work properly, while hardware is often designed to run special software.

hardware

software

The Basic Parts

There are many different kinds of computers, but common computers called desktop computers share the same basic parts. The main hardware of a computer is usually in the system case. It's connected to a screen called a monitor, which displays what the computer is doing.

A keyboard is used to type letters or other commands, and a mouse is used to click on objects to complete tasks. A mouse and keyboard are examples of input devices, which help the user tell the computer what to do.

The different parts of a computer are connected using cables. These cables, which have small wires inside them, carry information and commands to and from each computer part.

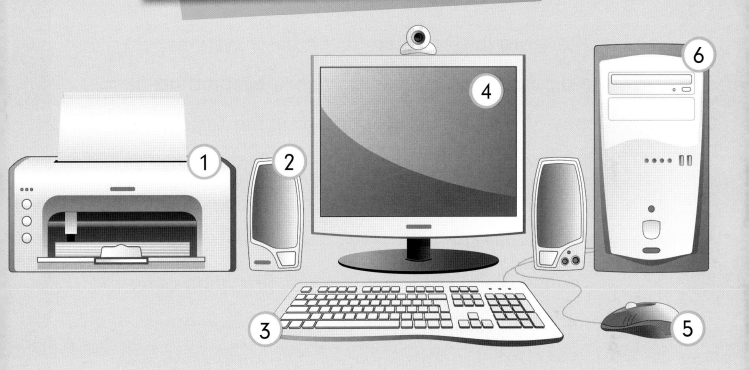

1. printer   2. speaker   3. keyboard   4. monitor   5. mouse   6. system case

Building Blocks

A cell phone or tablet computer has the same parts as a desktop computer, but in different forms. Tablets are one big monitor, but a touch screen acts as a mouse, and part of the screen can become a keyboard.

Talking to Mother

There are lots of different computer systems inside a system case. These parts are **assembled** at a factory. The most important piece in the system case is called the motherboard. This is a computer chip that lets the other chips and systems communicate with, or talk to, one another.

The motherboard is put in place first, then other systems are added and connected later. Some motherboards are different sizes. Computer engineers make sure the system case and other parts of the computer are compatible, or able to work together.

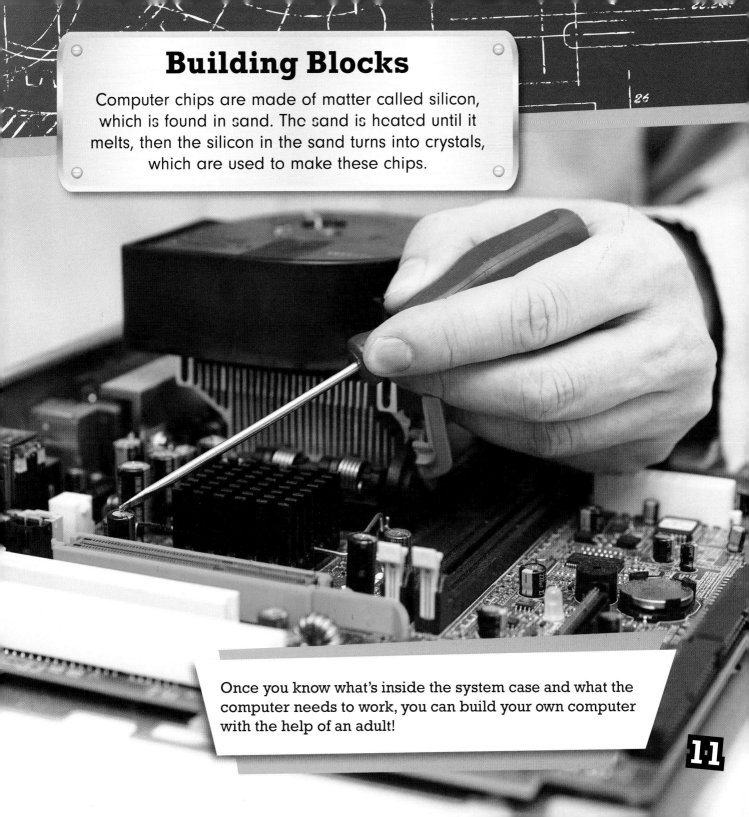

Building Blocks

Computer chips are made of matter called silicon, which is found in sand. The sand is heated until it melts, then the silicon in the sand turns into crystals, which are used to make these chips.

Once you know what's inside the system case and what the computer needs to work, you can build your own computer with the help of an adult!

Hard Storage

Next, the hard drive is **installed**. The hard drive is used to store memory. The computer's OS, programs, and other important information are stored on a hard drive. It's connected to the motherboard so other hardware can communicate with it.

There are different kinds of hard drives. Solid-state storage (SSD) uses electronics to save memory to a disc. Spinning hard-drive discs, called HDDs, use magnets to save memory to a disc. SSD is considered safer because if an HDD's magnets get harmed, memory can be lost.

SSD

Some computers also have drives called compact discs (CDs) that are used to read or store information like programs, music, and data.

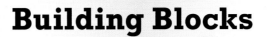

HDD

Every computer needs storage so the computer knows how it should run. Hard drives also save music, movies, and other useful things you want to use a computer for.

CPUs and Cooling

The central processing unit, or CPU, controls and executes, or carries out, all the commands a computer needs to work. The CPU is added to the motherboard after the hard drive. It rests on a base that lets it communicate with all other parts of the computer.

The CPU, hard drives, and motherboard all make lots of heat when they're working. Special fans and other cooling devices are added to computers to make sure their parts don't get too hot.

Building Blocks

The motherboard also has connections to the video and sound cards, which allow programs to run smoothly and let you listen to music or play video games. The motherboard also has a **sensor** that measures temperature.

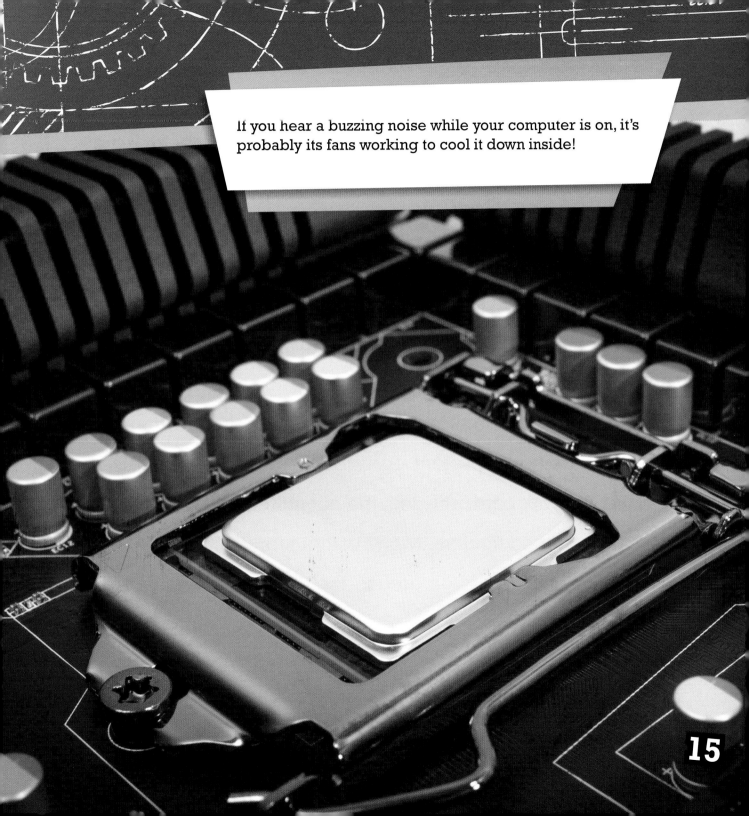

If you hear a buzzing noise while your computer is on, it's probably its fans working to cool it down inside!

15

RAM and Networks

Computers also need a different kind of memory to work properly. Called random-access memory, or RAM, it's also called **temporary** memory. Unlike the hard drive, RAM only stores memory while a computer is powered on. It's used by the CPU to store commands and other information needed for a computer to run.

Another important part added to the computer is the network card. This lets the computer communicate with other computers. Many computers use the Internet to send messages all around the world.

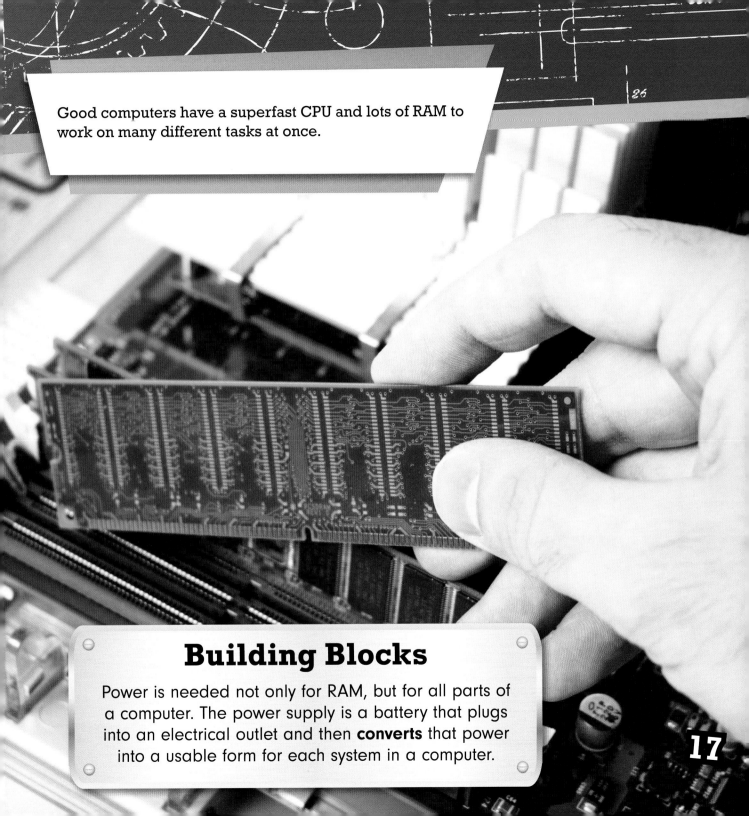

Good computers have a superfast CPU and lots of RAM to work on many different tasks at once.

Building Blocks

Power is needed not only for RAM, but for all parts of a computer. The power supply is a battery that plugs into an electrical outlet and then **converts** that power into a usable form for each system in a computer.

17

Final Testing

Some computers have more than one hard drive or different types of storage, which are also added at the factory. Once the basic parts of a computer are put in place, the system case is closed up and the computer is almost done.

Software is usually added to computers so they can be used right away. Before computers are sent off to the store, they're tested to make sure both the hardware and software work properly.

Building Blocks

Some companies let you order your own special computer, which means you can get whatever you want inside! What would you want your **custom** computer to have inside?

Many computers are ordered online today, which helps the customization process.

Code Your Own

It might get a bit expensive to build your own computer, but if you already have a computer handy, you can make your own computer programs! Here are some websites you can visit to start computer coding today!

tynker.com — Tynker helps you make your own video games, program a robot, and do much more!

kidsruby.com — Ruby is a fun programming language that you can use to make all kinds of things.

Glossary

assemble: to put together

code: the strings of characters used to create commands and computer software

convert: to change from one form to another

custom: specially made by someone, or one of a kind

design: to create the pattern or shape of something

device: a tool used for a certain purpose

electronic: a tool that uses electricity to work

engineer: someone who is trained in the use or building of machines

install: to set up or put in service

programming: the commands needed to operate a computer

sensor: a tool that can detect changes in its surroundings, such as sound or temperature

temporary: working or lasting for only a short time

For More Information

Books

Severance, Charles R., and Kristin Fontichiaro. *Raspberry Pi*. Ann Arbor, MI: Cherry Lake Publishing, 2014.

Zuchora-Walske, Christine. *What's Inside My Computer?* Minneapolis, MN: Lerner Publications, 2016.

Websites

Making a Computer
instructables.com/id/Making-a-Computer
Learn more about how you can make your own computer here.

Raspberry Pi
raspberrypi.org/resources/learn
Find out how you can make your own devices using Raspberry Pi parts here.

Index